Original title:
The Watch and the Stars

Copyright © 2025 Creative Arts Management OÜ
All rights reserved.

Author: Evan Hawthorne
ISBN HARDBACK: 978-1-80586-177-5
ISBN PAPERBACK: 978-1-80586-649-7

Celestial Patterns Unfolding

The moon forgot her shine, oh dear,
In day's bright light, she shed a tear.
The stars play hide and seek each night,
While comets dance in silly flight.

Big dipper spills its milk, so sweet,
While planets twirl on disco feet.
A cosmic jester, they delight,
As planets giggle, oh what a sight!

Celestial Mechanisms

One clock ticked loud, another went 'pop!',
Time's jigsaw puzzle flipped and hopped.
The sun, a chef, burns toast each day,
While shadows puddle up and play.

Galaxies spin like a feathered top,
As meteors play the hopscotch bop.
Tick-tock's laughter spills through the night,
While space-time dances with sheer delight.

Timeless Shadows Against Infinite Light

Shadows sneaking like mischievous cats,
Playing tag with twinkling hats.
Eclipses teasing, winking bright,
While astronauts prepare for a food fight.

The galaxies giggle in starlit suits,
As quasars bounce in moonlit boots.
A cosmic circus, what a thrill,
As the void ponders how to chill.

The Stars' Timeless Watch

A starlet yawns, then takes a bite,
Of stardust cookies, oh what a sight!
While meteors crack jokes with glee,
In a universe full of comedy.

Orion flexes, showing his brawn,
While Venus hums a silly dawn.
Time unfurls with a cheeky grin,
As galaxies swirl, let the fun begin!

Moments Beyond the Horizon

In a garden where shadows play,
The tulips dance in disarray.
A squirrel steals a wristwatch's shine,
While birds gossip over cheap red wine.

A cat counts the ticks with a frown,
As clouds wear silly hats upside down.
The sun winks, takes a playful bow,
While time slips like pudding from the cow.

Timekeepers of the Silver Sky

A clock with legs runs in the race,
Chasing dreams in a furry lace.
The moon grins with a cheesy glow,
Giggles burst from the stars below.

A calendar breaks in laughter loud,
As minutes giggle, proudly bowed.
An owl with glasses reads the night,
Advises all to take it light!

A Symphony of Night and Time

The cuckoo sings a silly tune,
While crickets dance beneath the moon.
A mouse conducts with tiny paws,
While fireflies flash in loud applause.

The moon's a chef, cooking starlight,
And laughter bubbles in the night.
Each tick and tock a burst of glee,
As time hops on a trampoline!

Luminous Secrets of the Cosmos

In a starry hall of tricks and fun,
Comets race til the morning sun.
A space cat drags a cosmic snack,
While planets dance in a silly pack.

Galaxies spin in a conga line,
Floating on custard, feeling fine.
While aliens giggle and play charades,
Time flies on a skateboard, no parades!

Time's Illuminated Path

Tick-tock, I lost my shoe,
Running late, oh what a view!
Hands are spinning, can't keep track,
Maybe next week, I'll get it back.

Racing clocks with every bounce,
Time's a jester, watch it flounce!
Hours take naps while I dance,
In this waltz, I miss my chance!

When Seconds Meet the Universe

Seconds attempt to cut a deal,
With galaxies, they want to feel.
A cosmic wink, then off they go,
Leaving me here with a toe to toe.

Counting stars, I lost my plot,
Wishing for a twinkle not forgot.
They laugh at me from far above,
Oh, how they dance, my lost love!

Chasing Celestial Whispers

Whispers rush like comet tails,
Tickling my ears with silver trails.
I chase them down, but they just giggle,
In this chase, my feet do wiggle.

Planets chuckle as I tumble,
My cosmic dance is quite the jumble!
Voices echo, 'Catch us, please!'
Oh, the fun of heavenly tease!

The Rhythm of Distant Lights

Distant lights throw a funky party,
While I'm stuck here feeling smarty.
They boogie down, I try to groove,
But I just end up in a move!

Stars flicker like a disco ball,
While I trip and nearly fall.
Counting beats, I lose my rhythm,
Ah, why do lights need such a schism?

Nighttime's Celestial Embrace

The moon wears shades, oh what a sight,
It winks at me, in the cloak of night.
Stars are twinkling, having a ball,
I ask the sky, 'Who's the superstar?'

Jupiter's laughing, what a big guy,
While Venus dances, oh my, oh my!
I trip on constellations, lose my shoe,
The Big Dipper flings it right back too!

Beyond Time's Familiar Path

Tick-tock goes the clock, who needs a guide?
When hours are made of candy, let's take a ride!
Yesterday's jokes, still fresh like a stew,
Time's just a prankster, pulling tricks anew.

I asked a sundial, it smirked with grace,
Said, 'Dude, I'm just here to slow the pace!'
With every second, a giggle or two,
Who knew time could play peek-a-boo?

A Symphony of Light and Moments

A comet zooms by, like it's late for tea,
While the stars harmonize, sipping on brie.
Nebulas burst, in colors loud and bright,
Who knew a galaxy could party all night?

Planets play tag, round and round they go,
While a black hole munches on an old photo.
They all laugh together, what a cosmic cheer,
Not one cares about the end of the year!

Flickers of Time Under Stellar Canopies

Under the sky, we share a great snack,
Counting the stars, there's no one to lack.
I tossed a wish, it hit a tree,
The branches chuckled, just like me!

A shooting star zoomed by, what a tease,
It tripped on a cloud, said, 'Excuse me, please!'
We giggled together, in our dreamy parade,
Flickers of joy, in the night, they invade!

Letters from the Infinite

I wrote a note to the cosmos bright,
Hoping the stars would write back tonight.
They sent me a wink, a twinkling tease,
I think they're just busy, sipping on cheese.

I asked for a guide, a stellar GPS,
But all I got was a cosmic mess.
They claimed to be lost, floating like ducks,
Next time I'll ask for a map, just my luck!

I pleaded for wisdom, a thread in the void,
But all I received was an intergalactic ploy.
"Just make a wish on a comet," they said,
Amused, I replied, "And what if I'm misled?"

So here I sit, laughing at fate,
With notes to the heavens, just tempting my fate.
The universe giggles, in silence it beams,
Maybe it's just chuckling at silly dreams.

Tales Written in Light

Once upon a comet, zooming past fast,
A gentleman star had a party aghast.
With asteroids dancing and meteors jazz,
They lost their twinkle—oh, what a razz!

A tale spun in stardust, a riddle of fun,
They laughed until light seemed to run.
"Who needs a planet? We've got this glow!"
"Just watch your step, or off we might go!"

The sun wore sunglasses, a jaunty flair,
While planets played truth or dare in midair.
The moon flipped pancakes while Saturn made tea,
"Next year, let's invite the black hole!" said he.

As stories unraveled, both silly and bright,
They shimmered together, delighting in light.
For who would have thought, in the theater vast,
The funniest tales in the cosmos amassed?

Reflections in Cosmic Waters

Down by the puddles of a cosmic stream,
The galaxies flashed like a wild, wild dream.
The ripples giggled, bouncing up high,
"Did you see that? A comet just flew by!"

I dipped my toe in, just for a peek,
It splashed a whole nebula, made the stars squeak!
"Hey, kid, watch it! We're swimming in light!"
I stammered, "Sorry, just thought it felt right!"

The sun teased the moon, "Let's race for a laugh!"
While Martians debated their favorite giraffe.
In spaces so vast, all the fun could be found,
Even black holes joined, spinning round and round.

So if you're ever bored, feel free to roam,
In cosmic waters, find a new home.
Just don't make a splash that's too grandiose,
Or you might just tickle a stellar ghost!

The Moon's Whispered Secrets

At midnight, the moon confesses in beams,
Of alien snacks and their silly schemes.
"I tried to bake cookies, but they turned to gas,
Now Saturn's all giddy, and I'm stuck with grass!"

Whispers of Venus, oh so divine,
Said, "Let's throw a party, with stardust wine!"
But Earth just rolled eyes, with a sigh of despair,
"Last time you hosted, there was dust everywhere!"

A turtle shot by, on a rocket, so spry,
"How do I land?!" he simply asked the sky.
So the moon just laughed, that old cheeky sprite,
"Just slow it down, and you'll glide through the night!"

With giggles and chuckles, the night draped with glee,
Cosmic friends shared secrets beneath the old tree.
And who would have thought, in the glittering lore,
That laughter and stardust were worth so much more?

The Infinite Dance of Time

Tick-tock goes the silly clock,
It dances around like a feathery sock.
Minutes waltz, hours jiggle,
Time's a party, just add a giggle.

A second slips, oh what a tease,
It makes us chase like a sneeze in the breeze.
Backwards or forwards, it loves to play,
Time's got moves; hip hip hooray!

Here comes noon with a cheeky grin,
Says, 'Join the fun, let the madness begin!'
Chasing shadows, leaping light,
Dancing in circles, oh what delight.

And when the clock strikes, cats go wild,
Time takes a break, just like a child.
So let us twirl till the sun says bye,
In this dance of time, we'll reach for the sky.

Spheres of Creation

Planets spin like marbles on a track,
Rolling around in their cosmic snack.
With each twirl, they hum a tune,
In this grand ballet beneath the moon.

Galaxies toss like spaghetti in space,
A swirling mess, oh what a race!
Stars wink at us, playful and bright,
As we laugh at their twinkling light.

Look out for comets, they dash and zoom,
Whipping past like brooms in a room.
Space is silly, a vast, funny show,
Where time flies fast, but we take it slow.

So grab a seat and enjoy the ride,
In this funky universe, there's nowhere to hide.
With laughter in tow and joy in our hearts,
We dance through the spheres, where fun never departs.

Echoes of a Celestial Clock

A clock on a hill, its face full of cheese,
Ticking away like a swarm of buzzing bees.
Each chime is a giggle, a tickle, a toot,
Echoing laughter from a raucous flute.

Time wears a hat, a comical sight,
Spinning and twirling, it's out for a night.
Echoes ring out, "Don't take this so slow!,"
As we bop to the rhythm, let the silliness flow.

Hours dance by in a pirouette,
Making us chuckle, and no time to fret.
Minutes can prance like they're on a spree,
In the grand echo chamber, we're wild and free.

So let's embrace the giggles of fate,
With a celestial tickle, let's celebrate.
As the echoes of laughter fill the clock's big face,
We'll bounce through our time in this whimsical place.

Interstellar Journeys Through Time

Rockets zooming, off we go,
Through cosmic giggles, we glide, and flow.
Time is a boomerang, back it will come,
Swirling around like a silly drum.

Spaceships beep with a beep-beep roar,
Twirling through comets, we ask for more.
Each light year dances, a skip and a hop,
In this vast playground, we never stop!

With aliens laughing, and stars that pop,
We'll chart out our fun with a zany never drop.
Time stretches and folds like a rubbery band,
In interstellar frolics, we're perfectly planned.

So wave goodbye to the mundane and tau,
Let's orbit around in our own magic wow.
In the interstellar sway, let's bubble and gleam,
In a journey of laughter, we chase every dream.

The Clocktower's Cosmic Chime

In a tower tall, the bells go ding,
They chime with joy, and make us sing.
Time does hop like a froggy friend,
Ticking and tocking, it never does end.

The hands are dancing, oh what a sight,
Spinning around in the pale moonlight.
Each tick a joke, each tock a pun,
Laughing at time, we'll never outrun.

People pause, and then they stare,
As hours twirl in a cosmic glare.
Jesters of time with silly faces,
Chasing the past in comical races.

So let them chime, let laughter ensue,
Ticking away all the worries we brew.
In this tower of fun, let the minutes play,
And trip through the cosmos, come what may.

In the Shadow of Luminescent Dreams

Beneath the glow of a silly moon,
Stars stumble around, a cosmic tune.
Dreams take flight on fluffy clouds,
Whispering secrets to overly loud crowds.

The night wears giggles like a fine gown,
As dreams pinch the sleepy from their frown.
With each twinkle a wink, so rude,
Cosmic mischief in a humor-filled mood.

Laughter echoes in the dreamy night,
Chasing shadows that giggle in fright.
Falling stars slip on banana peels,
Making wishes with playful squeals.

In the realm of dreams, all is absurd,
Where funny thoughts freely stirred.
So laugh with the stars, let your heart beam,
In the glow of night, we'll weave a dream.

Celestial Dial of Destiny

Spin the wheel of fate, if you dare,
With cosmic dial, life's a fair.
Planets wobble, galaxies spin,
Time's silly dance invites us in.

To chart our course through humorous space,
With puppy dog stars leading the race.
Laughing as comets come zooming by,
With goofy grins, oh me, oh my!

Who knew that destiny's just a jest?
Each plan a punchline, each dream a quest.
Floating through life with giggles galore,
We write our tales and then we roar.

So let's embrace this humorous ride,
With laughter in heart, let giggles collide.
In this cosmic circus, we'll find our way,
With every chuckle, come what may.

The Astral Pendulum

A pendulum swings in a cosmic dance,
Tickling the space in a whimsical trance.
Each swing a laugh, each tick a cheer,
Time's little joke is always near.

Astronauts chuckle as they float about,
In zero-g, there's never a doubt.
Every second brings a silly surprise,
With stars shaking hands, oh what a prize!

Cosmic clocks are mischief at play,
Juggling moments in a funny way.
As planets giggle in their orbits wide,
We chase the giggles, we take the ride.

So let the pendulum sway and swing,
With heart made light, let laughter ring.
In this marvelous mess, we dance along,
Swaying through time, with a humorous song.

Celestial Silhouettes

In the sky a big spoon, I see,
Guess it's for soup, oh, woe is me.
Stars are just tiny, shiny sprouts,
Who knew they'd bring such silly bouts?

Comets eat popcorn, zoom around,
Giggling with meteors, playful sound.
Every twinkle's like a wink, I swear,
Heavens have humor, floating in air.

Aliens in space having a feast,
Nibbling on planets, the cosmic beast.
Their spaceship's a taco, oh what a sight,
Bouncing through orbits, day turns to night.

Jupiter's dancing, Saturn's a clown,
While Earth looks puzzled, wearing a frown.
In this cosmic circus, we try our best,
Laughing and joking, it's a funny quest.

Stargazed Hours

Counting stars as if they were sheep,
Lost in dreams, oh what a leap.
Galaxies twist like a noodle well,
Slurping up light, oh what the hell!

Meteors race, but one trips on fate,
Spilling its candy, oh how late!
While wise old owls hoot from the trees,
They giggle at comets bursting like peas.

Looking for aliens—what a disgrace,
One looks back with a pie on its face.
Cosmic pizza's flying through the sky,
Take a slice quick, don't be shy!

As sunrises peek like a curious cat,
Stars are now sleeping, imagine that!
With winks and smiles, the night's now a whirl,
In this silly dance of the cosmic pearl.

Time's Fateful Call

Tick-tock goes the clock, it's a prank!
Time's got a sense of humor, gives thanks.
Minute hands waltz with the hour too,
Shuffling their feet in a ridiculous view.

The sundial's blushing, it's quite a sight,
Burnt from the sun in the broad daylight.
While the old cuckoo starts to snore,
Making the seconds, feel like a chore.

Every tick is a joke, every tock, a pun,
What if time's just playing? Oh, what fun!
Calendar pages flipping with cheer,
"Where did the days go?"—the answer's unclear.

So dance with the hours, don't take a fall,
Join the clock's party, let's have a ball.
With laughter and joy, let's shout and sing,
For time's fateful call is a funny thing!

The Constellation Chronicles

Once upon a twinkle in the night,
Shapes took the stage, what a funny sight!
A bear with a hat, tripping on stars,
Lost in the cosmos, dodging guitars.

A hunter's lost his bow, oh dear me,
It's rolling away, like a runaway bee.
While a fish does the cha-cha with flair,
In this starlit theatre, nothing's unfair.

A wallaby whispers to a nearby moon,
"Let's disco dance—come on, let's croon!"
As planets laugh, orbiting wide,
In this cosmic tale, let humor abide!

So sketch your dreams on the celestial sea,
With giggles and chuckles, it's plain to see.
Every star shines bright, with tales to share,
In the constellation chronicles, laughter is rare!

Clocks and Constellations Collide

Tick-tock giggles from the clock,
While Mars dons a silly sock.
Jupiter dances on a whim,
As light years sneak a little peek at him.

Second hands twist like a curly fry,
While stars wink with a cheeky eye.
A minute moon makes funny faces,
In the cosmic ballet of silly places.

Laughter echoes in the night,
As clocks chime in delight.
Galaxies spin with a twist of fate,
While time plays tag, it's never late.

Radiance of Ancient Timers

Old clocks creak like a rusty door,
Tickling seconds we can't ignore.
Galactic giggles fill the air,
As constellations play truth or dare.

The Big Dipper trips on its tail,
While timekeepers tell a silly tale.
A comet crashes with a puff of smoke,
As laughter rings out from every stroke.

Each tick like a prank in open space,
While celestial bodies have a race.
Yeah, time may fly, but so do we,
Chasing laughs across the cosmic sea.

Navigating Through Stars and Seconds

Navigating time with a wink and grin,
Where seconds dance and stars begin.
A sundial blinks and then it laughs,
For each tick adds to the cosmic gaffs.

Navigators glance with a silly glee,
As galaxies twirl with jubilee.
Time takes a break, calls out for fun,
While meteors race just to be done.

In this odd game of cosmic chess,
A clock smirks, feeling quite blessed.
Stars throw confetti up in delight,
As moments tumble into the night.

Galaxy's Timeless Serenade

A serenade drifts from afar,
As clocks strum chords with a twinkling star.
In cosmic concert, they join in play,
With melodies that tickle night and day.

Silly shadows dance on Mars,
Timekeepers giggle while counting stars.
The moon throws a party, wild and free,
While seconds skip like a playful bee.

In this galaxy's ball, waltzing in sync,
Time doesn't ponder, it's quick on the brink.
Round and around, oh what a tease,
As laughter and stardust float on the breeze.

The Celestial Calendar

Twinkle lights chase tiny cats,
In the night where whimsy chats.
Counting time with a silly grin,
As gravity pulls us all to spin.

A cow jumped over, quite the sight,
While aliens dance with delight.
Calendars say I'm late again,
But who needs time? I'm busy then!

Rabbits leap in swirling skies,
Chasing shadows, saying goodbyes.
Oh, what fun to lose track of days,
In this cosmic, silly maze!

I tried to eat a dream last night,
It tasted weird, not quite right.
Stars giggle at my sleepy head,
While comets whisper, "Go to bed!"

Flickering Memories of the Infinite

Flickering lights in funny streams,
Where memories swim like silly dreams.
A glass of joy spills on the floor,
And laughter drifts out through the door.

Time winks out from the clock's big face,
While squirrels plot their next big race.
I used to chase the moving moon,
But tripped instead and fell on a tune!

A time machine? I'm building one,
With a rubber band and a lot of fun.
I'll fly to lunch in 1960,
But end up stuck with a rubber sticky!

Chasing shadows that dance and play,
I lose myself in a cosmic ballet.
With giggles floating in the dark,
In this infinite, silly park!

Time's Enchanted Orbit

Round and round like a merry-go,
Time spins fast, oh what a show!
A giggling sun with a cheeky grin,
Invites the stars to come dance in.

Planets hula in a cosmic race,
Oh the joy that fills this place!
Comets zoom with a wink and smile,
While space-time tangos a silly mile.

Caffeine-fueled astronauts float with glee,
Telling tales of where they have to be.
But drift away on a cosmic spree,
With giggles echoing, "Just wait for me!"

In orbits drawn with crayons bright,
We scribble dreams under the moonlight.
Time's enchanting in its playful style,
So let's lose track and stay awhile!

Beneath the Canopy of Twilight

Under skies that wear a smile,
We gather here for a little while.
Twilight giggles in shades of blue,
While shadows play peek-a-boo!

Silly owls hoot a midnight tune,
As crickets plot a disco, too.
Stars drape the night in sequined gowns,
While the moon wears its favorite crown.

Every firefly with its glowing spree,
Whispers secrets to a buzzing bee.
As night unfolds its whimsical charms,
Time forgets us in its arms.

So let's dance beneath this twinkling dome,
In a realm where laughter roams.
With every tick, I trip and fall,
Yet love indeed – this time after all!

Gaze of the Timeless Traveler

A traveler with a ticking face,
Looks at the sky, in a merry race.
The stars are winking, quite a sight,
While he checks his time, day and night.

He whispers to Jupiter, "What's the time?"
And gets a giggle, "You're out of your prime!"
"Your clock's turning funny, oh what a hoot!"
"Just follow the twinkle, you silly old brute!"

With a leap and a bound, he jumps to the moon,
"Is naptime coming, or just a cartoon?"
The sun gives a grin, in a playful burn,
"Tick-tock, dear friend, it's your turn to learn!"

So he dances along in a cosmic ballet,
With stars chuckling softly, as they sway.
Time's just a joke, can you see it so clear?
Laughing with planets, our traveler dear.

Cosmic Hourglass

An hourglass floats in the void of dark,
Filled with stardust, it sends a spark.
I flipped it once, then flipped it twice,
Now I'm stuck waiting, like a game of dice.

A comet rolled by, making a fuss,
Said, "Time's just a notion, come ride on the bus!"
The bus is on a route of bright shooting stars,
Let's laugh over coffee, on Luna's bizarre.

I spilled a drop in the sands of time,
And the hourglass grinned, "You've broken a rhyme!"
With every grain, I chuckled and sighed,
Why is it always a joyride to glide?

So let's make some noise in the silence of space,
With jokes and confetti, we'll win the race.
Tick-tock may confound, but it's all in jest,
In the cosmic hourglass, we have the best.

Eclipsing Moments

When the moon plays coy, hiding the sun,
Moments eclipse in a playful run.
"Hey there!" calls Venus, "You're blocking the light!"
"Just hold on tight, it'll be quite a sight!"

Laughter erupts from a nearby star,
"Check out the shadows, we're going far!"
Each flicker of darkness shimmers with joy,
While planets spin tales like a celestial toy.

Time takes a break, just to share a grin,
"Eclipsing moments, let the fun begin!"
With colors that dance in a cosmic parade,
The sun and the moon trade jokes unafraid.

When twilight fades, and giggles grow wide,
The universe cheers, it can't be denied.
With joy upon joy, in this stellar zoom,
We laugh at the chaos, in rendezvous bloom.

Starlit Rhythm of Life

In the rhythm of twinkles, we jiggle along,
With a heartbeat of stardust, we dance like a song.
"Is it time for a snack?" Jupiter would coo,
As Mars brings the chips, all coated in dew.

The rhythm keeps changing, like a cosmic DJs,
With beats from Saturn taking up space.
Each star struts in, it's a sight to behold,
With fireflies wearing outfits of gold.

"Oops, tripped on a comet!" laughter would crash,
As meteors shoot by, in a glittery flash.
Time is a joker, with jokes on repeat,
In the starlit ballroom, we two-step and greet.

So let's spin 'round the orbits, with giggles to share,
In the dance of forever, without a care.
With the cosmos in sync, let the fun thrive,
For life's just a waltz, with stars alive!

Twilight's Counting Heartbeats

As the sun dips low, time takes a break,
A squirrel steals my sandwich, oh what a mistake!
Crickets begin their nightly ballet,
While I sip my lemonade, dreaming away.

With every tick, there's a giggle or two,
A frog leaps by, wearing shoes made of glue.
Stars start to twinkle, but I can't stay awake,
Counting them all feels like a piece of cake.

A cat starts to yawn, the moon's fierce gaze,
Telling me tales of the magical bays.
I let out a chuckle, as fireflies dance,
In this silly twilight, it's a cosmic romance.

As minutes waltz by, slipping through the night,
I trip on my shoelace, oh what a sight!
Yet in this laughter, our worries take flight,
Embracing the moments, all feels just right.

The Illumination of Passing Minutes

My clock is a joker, it chuckles with glee,
It spins in circles, playing tricks on me.
With every chime, it puffs out a puff,
Saying, 'Hurry up! You're just not fast enough!'

The moon is a mischievous ol' pal,
Winks at the sun with a grin and a cowl.
Time slips and slides on banana peels,
While my cat juggles stars with impressive squeals.

Old trees gossip with rustling leaves,
While I'm here wondering, 'Where are my keys?'
Each moment dragged by like molasses in flight,
Yet laughter holds strong in this wobbly night.

I chuckle at seconds that tiptoe around,
As puddles reflect every sound—what a sound!
In the theater of night, absurd and bright,
I find joy in moments til the dawn's first light.

Temporal Trails Through the Milky Way

Chasing the minutes on cosmic roller skates,
Zooming through space, no time for debates.
A comet wearing glasses zooms by with a wink,
While stars make confetti—oh, what do you think?

The planets throw parties, each one quite a scene,
Dancing in circles, they're all looking keen.
Saturn serves punch from its rings made of fun,
Who knew that space could be this well done?

Meteor showers rain down like sprinkles,
Shooting stars giggle, leaving only crinkles.
I reach for a bite of my celestial pie,
With each passing moment, I can't help but sigh.

Laughter erupts as black holes make noise,
Swirling our snacks 'til they're just little toys.
In this wild galaxy, I truly feel gay,
As I revel in time—come what may!

Galaxy's Silent Countdown

In a world upside down, the countdown begins,
Where pancakes fly high and gravity grins.
A star on a diet turns out to be vain,
Always counting calories, never the gain.

Off in the distance, a rocket learns yoga,
Struggling to stretch, it spins like a hoga.
While asteroids giggle, all bumpy and loud,
In the dance of the cosmos, they float like a cloud.

Time ticks unbothered, it holds no regrets,
While comets debate their best hairstyles and pets.
I sit back and chuckle at this galactic show,
As laughter complies with what we don't know.

All around the void, there's joy in the air,
For even in silence, we find what we share.
With every heartbeat, the universe sways,
Embracing the beauty of our quirky days.

A Vault of Shimmering Memories

In the attic, dust bunnies play,
Chasing memories from yesterday.
Grandma's clock ticks, what a joke,
Why does it sound like a silly poke?

Shiny trinkets spill from the chest,
Each one claims to know what's best.
Twirling globes and jiggly toys,
What a show, oh what a noise!

The old lamp flickers, doing the dance,
As if it knows it's our last chance.
Whispers of laughter fill the air,
Echoing secrets we all still share.

Under the sunbeam, time does waltz,
Juggling moments, its playful vaults.
With every tick, another tale spins,
In a vault where laughter begins!

Time's Celestial Canvas

Brush of time on the cosmic stage,
Painting patterns, oh what a rage!
Stars twinkle like winking eyes,
They must have secrets, oh what a guise!

In the garden of tick-tock trees,
Laughter hangs, swaying in the breeze.
Pebbles dance, calling to the moon,
Crooning a silly cosmic tune.

Comets race with candy-like tails,
Shooting giggles through cosmic trails.
Eons pass like a cat's meow,
"Where's the time?" we all ask now!

Wondrous whimsy all around,
In this space where laughs abound!
Every twinkle, a joke to find,
On this canvas, silly and blind.

The Heritage of Cosmic Wonders

Inheritances from stars so bright,
Cosmic wonders, a comical sight.
Stars sharing jokes through blackened night,
"Don't trust planets, they're not quite right!"

Galaxies giggle in swirling spins,
With every twirl, they tickle the sins.
Dust clouds whisper secrets of bold,
What treasures they offer, if only told!

Falling asteroids, what a silly race,
Each with styles, a dressed-up grace.
Shooting stars snicker as they zoom,
"Catch us if you can, doom and gloom!"

Through this heritage of laughs and plays,
Cosmos enjoys its merry ways.
Every blink, a jest unfurled,
In the laughter of this endless world!

Tides of Cosmic Time

Waves of time roll like ocean tides,
Ticking treasures where fun resides.
Forecast of laughter fills the sky,
As chickens dance and horses fly!

Under the moon, shadows take a leap,
Making funny shapes before we sleep.
Stars giggle at our puzzled frowns,
Winking down on upside-down towns.

Galactic waves rhythmically sway,
In the grand cosmic ballet.
"Time is a joke," they seem to shout,
Rolling in laughter, without a doubt!

Navigating dreams upon this sea,
Every wave singing, "Join us, be free!"
In the tides where the merry reside,
Floating on giggles, let's enjoy the ride!

Stitching Stars in Celestial Fabrics

In the night sky, I sew with flair,
Threading comets without a care.
My needle's sharp, my fabric wide,
Creating patterns where dreams collide.

Meteors crash, a wobbly sight,
They dance and twirl, oh what a night!
Galaxies giggle, twinkling small,
While I stitch on, not shocked at all.

Nebulas rustle, nervous they seem,
Afraid I'll snip their cosmic dream.
I promise, dear fluff, you're safe with me,
Just keep spinning in harmony.

Amidst laughter, the void takes flight,
I craft my tales until daylight.
With every stitch, I share a jest,
In fabrics of night, I find my quest.

Cosmic Resonances

In a world of sound, the planets hum,
Their music plays—what a funny drum!
A melody of moons, with beats so strange,
Who knew the cosmos could rearrange?

Jupiter jumps, what an awkward move,
While Saturn spins, it tries to groove.
Uranus grins, a cheeky smile,
In this vast dance, we laugh all the while.

Shooting stars sneak in to serenade,
A cosmic chorus begins to parade.
With giggles shared and space-time bends,
This celestial party never ends.

Harmonies soar through the Milky Way,
Each planet joins in a cosmic play.
We'll laugh and sing, and twirl in glee,
In this universe, wild and free!

The Grains of Eternity

Grains of time tumble, what a clatter,
Slipping through fingers, like pizza batter.
A sprinkle of joy, a dash of mirth,
In this cosmic kitchen, we stir the Earth.

Each grain's a story, a giggle dust,
A testament to each silly thrust.
As clocks go round with hilarious ticks,
I'm stuck wondering, what's the next fix?

Laugh lines deepen in the sands of fate,
Wishing I'd packed a much lighter weight.
Time does a jig, it hops and prances,
While I chase grains, in clumsy dances.

Eternal tales in a bowl of stars,
Mixing laughter with Jupiter's jars.
We'll eat this moment, so rich and sweet,
With cosmic crumbs, oh, what a treat!

A Metronome of Celestial Light

Tick-tock, the universe swings wide,
Each second jumbles, it cannot hide.
A metronome laughs in rhythm so bright,
Counting stars, while we groove all night.

The moon spins 'round like a dizzy dancer,
While comets fly by in a playful prancer.
The sun cracks jokes, a fiery wit,
And even black holes chuckle a bit.

Galactic giggles echo around,
With every beat, a joy unbound.
From quasars to asteroids, all join in,
Making the universe laugh, oh what a win!

So here we groove, in this cosmic clock,
Tapping our toes to the light's sweet knock.
In laughter's embrace, we feel just right,
With each tick-tock of celestial light.

Glimmering Hours

Time winks at us from its perch,
Ticks and tocks in a silly lurch.
Minutes dance like they're on a spree,
While hours giggle, blissfully free.

In daylight's grasp, we chase the fun,
But twilight comes, and oh, what a run!
Each second bounces, we can't keep still,
As laughter echoes through every thrill.

The sun sets low, the shadows creep,
Time's playing tricks as we lose sleep.
With every tick, we're counting sheep,
The clock's a joker, our dreams it'll sweep.

So here we are, in this merry chase,
With whimsy and time, we share a space.
Life's fleeting moments, hilariously grand,
As hours flutter like grains of sand.

Constellations of Memory

In dreams, I find twinkling sights,
Nonsense thoughts in starry nights.
Comets zooming with silly flair,
While wishes bounce like they don't care.

Under the vast, bewildering sky,
I raise my hands and start to fly.
Each memory a star so bright,
Giggling past in the moon's soft light.

Galaxies twirl with a chuckle or two,
A cosmic joke that's drawn for you.
Nebulas bloom like cotton candy,
Every moment feels sweet and dandy.

As I drift in this comet's tail,
I laugh with the cosmos, I cannot fail.
Stars snicker softly, a whimsical launch,
In this universe, memories prance and paunch.

Eternal Echoes in the Night

The night sky hums a silly tune,
Echoing laughter from the moon.
Stars bob and weave, in playful mood,
With goofy grins, they make us food.

Shadows dance on the ground below,
While ticklish breezes start to blow.
Every giggle that fills the air,
Is a winking secret, a joyous dare.

Whispers of joy float through the trees,
Even crickets join in with glee.
With every chime, the night is bright,
In this timeless realm, all is light.

So let's frolic in midnight's embrace,
With echoes of laughter, let's find our place.
In this cosmic silliness, stars unite,
As the universe chuckles, all through the night.

The Clockwork of Heaven

In heavenly gears, the rhythms play,
Each second jostles in comical sway.
With cosmic cogs that sip their tea,
Time's a jester, oh can't you see?

Angels giggle in heavenly shifts,
Playing pranks with celestial gifts.
Their laughter chimes in silver tones,
Tickling hearts from high to drones.

Galaxies spin with a wink and a spin,
In this grand machine where fun begins.
Stars wear glasses, pretending to be wise,
While comets play tag in starry skies.

So join this dance in the sky's delight,
Where every tick brings bliss to the night.
In the clockwork of heaven, joy's the key,
As time and laughter spin endlessly free.

The Hourglass of Stardust

In a glass of sand so fine,
Time slips out, and I just whine.
I sneeze, and there go all those years,
Scattering stardust with my tears.

I thought I'd find a cosmic key,
But it's just a cat stuck in a tree!
Chasing time like it's a mouse,
I fall right through my own space house.

The grains of space are quite the prank,
They tickle me, then laugh and prank.
As I bumble through this astral dance,
I slip on moonbeams—no second chance!

So grab a wink from Saturn's ring,
Make wishes, let your laughter sing.
In this galactic silly race,
I'll take my time, my funny place.

Dreams Beneath the Cosmic Canopy

Under twinkling lights so bright,
Dreams make mischief, taking flight.
With every wish, a comet zooms,
And I trip over celestial brooms.

I thought I'd sail on starry beams,
But crashed instead in cosmic dreams.
Cosmos coffee spills on my face,
I'm now a nebula in disgrace!

Jupiter's storms play peek-a-boo,
While I juggle with the alien crew.
We laughed as they served up moon pie,
Then all agreed we'd like to fly!

But dreams do fade at dawn's first light,
I giggle and wave to the night.
So keep your dreams, let them expand,
For in this chaos, we'll take a stand!

The Universe's Gentle Tick

A clock that's lost its sense of time,
Ticks and tocks in rhythm, slime.
I chase the echoes of its beat,
Slipping on space cheese at my feet.

Galaxies wink as I make a fuss,
With cosmic socks upon the bus.
Each tick is paired with a little laugh,
As I plot my nonsensical path.

Sirius giggles, Orion's winks,
While I spill my interstellar drinks.
I try to dance with gravity's thread,
But float like jelly—oh, I'm misled!

So if you hear the universe chuckle,
Join in the fun, and embrace the shuffle.
For in the ticking, there's laughter fair,
Just watch your step in the cosmic air!

Lightyears Between Moments

Each moment stretches like taffy,
As I chase light at times quite chaffy.
A lightyear's laugh echoes through space,
Where every star has a silly face!

I stumbled on a comet's tail,
And opened up a galactic mail.
It fizzled out like a soda pop,
Exploding time, oh, what a flop!

While aliens juggle time like clowns,
I fumble through celestial towns.
But laughter travels at light speed,
Making moments bloom like wildweed!

So let's race through this cosmic bazaar,
From Jupiter's pie to fancy car.
With lightyears spread and joy in tow,
We'll trip through time with a silly glow!

Echoes of the Celestial Mechanism

In the night, a clock does tick,
While giggling stars play a trick.
Moonbeams weave through cosmic cheer,
They dance around, year after year.

A sundial laughs, it knows the game,
While hands of time adjust with fame.
Nebulas burst in clouds of fun,
As meteors streak, one by one.

A comet slips, a little shy,
It trips on light and waves goodbye.
The universe, a playground vast,
As moments fly, we hold them fast.

Time forgets to take a break,
In orbits wide, the stars do shake.
With laughter shared in cosmic space,
We chase the light, a gleeful race.

Beneath Eternity's Gaze

Beneath skies bright with winking eyes,
A calendar croaks with silly sighs.
It knows the dates, yet sings the wrong,
While constellations hum along.

A wrist adorned with twinkling gems,
Says 'Time's a joke', then bursts in hems!
Fleeting seconds, how they prance,
In cosmic rhythms, a quirky dance.

The planets waltz, the comets giggle,
As clocks tick on, they twist and wiggle.
Where seconds melt like ice cream scoops,
Galaxies burst into silly loops.

Eternity snickers, it's quite the puzzle,
As we juggle dreams in a cosmic hustle.
With laughter echoing through the spheres,
We toast to time and all our cheers!

Celestial Timekeepers

A turtle moon with a funny face,
Keeps track of time with a slow-paced grace.
Stars wear hats, and comets boast,
While minutes spin like a wild ghost.

A clock on Mars, oh what a sight,
It runs on chocolate and starlit spite.
The ticks and tocks, a rollicking song,
As planets giggle through the night long.

With each tick, a star takes flight,
Shooting off to frolic in light.
Jovial shadows cast by the sun,
In this realm, the laughter's never done.

Each cycle's punctuated with glee,
A cosmic jest, wild and free.
So let your hearts be a pendulum sway,
In the grand circus of night and day!

Twinkling Moments

Moments twinkle, like fairy wings,
Each one chirps as the starlight sings.
A wristwatch giggles, 'Oh, what a spree!'
As time flutters by, you just can't flee.

Meteor showers take a bow,
At lunar parties, offering a wow.
While calendars play hide and seek,
Joking around with each cheeky peak.

In cozy realms where laughter flies,
Suprising thrills emerge from skies.
Time is but a prankster in disguise,
Sowing joy in dreams that rise.

So chase the lights and dance with time,
In the theatre of space, it feels sublime.
As laughter echoes through each beat,
Moments twinkle, oh, they're sweet!

A Universe of Fleeting Moments

In my pocket a clock ticks away,
I chase after time like a playful stray.
Hours jump and dance, they find a way,
To sneak past my plans, oh what a day!

I spot a comet, it almost trips,
While planets all giggle, trading quips.
A wink from the moon, oh what a tease,
"Catch me if you can!" says the breeze.

Stars jive and twirl, in cosmic ballet,
While I miscalculate my lunch, by the way.
Time flies on wings, oh what a sight,
Life's just a jest, on this funny flight!

So here's to the moments, quick and bright,
That tickle our souls in the softest night.
We laugh in the dark, as comets zoom past,
In this universe of giggles, we're all unsurpassed!

Silent Echoes of Eternity

In the vastness a whisper, not quite a shout,
I trip over thoughts, what's this about?
Stars echo softly with humorous grace,
As I stumble and grin at the cosmic space.

Time takes a selfie, but it's blurry and bold,
The universe chuckles, "If only you were so old!"
I pirouette like stardust caught in a spin,
While laughter of galaxies pulls me right in.

"Why the long face?" asks a star with a wink,
As I try to remember my last decent drink.
Planets all giggle, meteors giggle too,
In this silent echo, they party for two.

So let's raise a toast to this timeless refrain,
Where laughs are the currency, and joy is the gain.
In the night's gentle hush, we make a fine crew,
Dancing through eternity, just me and you!

The Ticking Silence of the Void

Inside an empty space, a clock starts to tick,
But time is a jester, elusive and slick.
I check my wristwatch, it seems to conspire,
To keep me guessing, drawing me higher.

There's a silence that chuckles, a void full of pranks,
As stars roll their eyes at my timing misbanks.
"Are you lost, little traveler?" a comet inquires,
While I fumble for seconds, lost in my desires.

The silence erupts with a laughter so wide,
As I wonder where my silly socks could hide.
Banter with black holes, they gulp up my woes,
And giggle at how with laughter, life flows.

So let's tickle the void with our silly charms,
As time sprints away in a parade of alarms.
In the echoes of silence, humor unfurls,
Playing tag with the moments, in invisible swirls.

A Tapestry of Starry Nights

Stitching together each twinkling light,
I weave a tapestry of sheer delight.
Stars drop their needles, and laughter erupts,
While planets play games and life interrupts.

"How many wishes can fit in this sky?"
As I toss my coins, one slips right by.
Galaxies chuckle at my clumsy fate,
While I count the seconds, a humorous date.

The moon is a joker, with bright silver eyes,
As it pranks all the comets in playful disguise.
I join in the jest, under night's charming trick,
Where laughter's the treasure, and joy's the magic stick.

So let's dance through the cosmos, with silly delight,
In a world of strange wonders, we shine ever bright.
Creating a tapestry of whimsical sights,
In a jolly adventure of starry nights!

Whispers Across Time

Ticking away with a sense of glee,
Time winks at me like it's caught in a tree.
With every chime, it nudges my side,
Saying, 'I'm late for a cosmic ride!'

In this silly dance, we twirl and spin,
Around the sun, where laughter begins.
Chronicles tickle as they slip and slide,
Sending us giggling on the cosmic tide.

A calendar slips, its pages all torn,
It trips on a comet, oh what a scorn!
Yet laughter erupts from all space and time,
As clocks wear puns, and clocks feel sublime.

So let's watch the planets, with popcorn in tow,
As they play hide-and-seek in the starry domino!
Each tick is a joke, each tock a grand jest,
In the universe's comedy show, we're all blessed.

Journey Through the Astral Clock

Every second feels like a bumpy ride,
As planets align and begin to collide.
Twirling my way through the lunar bazaar,
Where time flies quicker than a speeding car!

My wrist just cracked like a cosmic whip,
As comets juggle and give time the slip.
Between spaces and giggles, I find my groove,
In this astral clock, we all make the move.

The Milky Way twinkles, a diamond so bright,
But what's this I hear? A tickling sprite!
"Hey! Who stole minutes?" cries the old sun,
Laughing loudly, saying, "It's all in good fun!"

Let's race through the cosmos, I challenge you first,
But don't trip on stardust or you might burst!
With laughter and joy, we'll count every jest,
In this timeless adventure, we're truly blessed!

The Pulse of Distant Worlds

Oh look! The planets have thrown a great bash,
With meteors dancing and planets that crash.
While quasars giggle in their radiant show,
And time runs in circles, fast, then slow.

Wormholes are winding, like spaghetti in space,
Tickling the comet's shiny little face.
As gravity pulls us into a whirl,
I check my pocket for a cosmic pearl!

Asteroids tumble, each one with a grin,
Throwing a party, let the fun begin!
With time as our DJ, spinning so fine,
We'll boogie through eons with a cheeky design.

Let's toast to the planets, oh what a delight,
As we dance through the cosmos, under the night.
In this pulse of worlds, laughter resounds,
In the heart of the sky, joy abounds.

Echoes in the Night

In the deep of the night, where laughter can soar,
Echoes of giggles knock at my door.
"Who's there?" I ask, as shadows unfold,
With whispers of secrets that never grow old.

The moon plays the piano, its keys made of light,
As stars join the chorus, delightful and bright.
Time is a jester, with tricks up its sleeves,
Making us chuckle as it pulls at our dreams.

"Hey, what's that sound?" I giggle with glee,
As galaxies flicker like bright jubilee.
Clocks join the party with a tick-tock dance,
Making the whole universe sway in a trance.

So let's laugh at the dark, let's howl at the sky,
With echoes of joy that never say goodbye.
For in this vast cosmos, with wonders so bright,
We'll enjoy every tick in the warm, starry night.

Celestial Timekeepers

In the sky, the tickers play,
Counting stars in a wacky way.
Cosmic hands that spin and swirl,
Joking with the time, they twirl.

One tickled star starts to giggle,
While another one does a little wiggle.
Their laughter echoes through the night,
Making time feel feather-light.

A lunar clock with a sunny face,
Saying, 'Chill! We've all got space!'
Time stands still, or maybe not,
Who cares? There's fun right on the spot!

So here's to hours that tip and tease,
While comets dance with effortless ease.
In this cosmos, nothing's a bore,
Time and space forever explore.

Midnight's Whispered Secrets

At midnight, secrets start to creep,
While the universe tries not to sleep.
Whispers float on cosmic waves,
Of silly times and quirky braves.

A comet blinks, like a playful star,
Saying, 'Catch up, you won't go far!'
The moon chuckles at the hour,
Growing brighter, wielding its power.

Galaxies gossip, sharing tales,
Of hapless moons and dancing gales.
Time laughs so hard, it nearly spills,
Shooting stars fulfill our thrills.

In the silence where magic gleams,
Midnight holds all our wildest dreams.
With every tick, let joy ignite,
Secrets of the night take flight!

When Clocks Align with Constellations

When the dials align with the night,
Silly shadows dance in delight.
Tick-tock laughter fills the air,
As stardust shimmies without a care.

A clock with arms spins in a whirl,
While stars giggle and softly twirl.
Timing jokes like shooting stars,
"Can't catch me, I'm too far!"

Each constellation plays its part,
In this odd celestial art.
With every hour, the fun unrolls,
Time's cosmic caper pulls at our souls.

So let's join in, give a cheer,
For alignments that bring us near.
The night's a party, stars and clocks,
Dancing together, time paradox!

Observing Time's Cosmic Dance

In the void, a ballet unfolds,
Where time and stars share jokes untold.
Planets pirouette, bright and bold,
While clocks tick-tock in the cold.

A meteor laughs as it zooms by,
Saying, 'Hold on tight, don't be shy!'
Laughter echoes, a stellar song,
Every second feels like a throng.

The sun takes a break with a wink,
As comets prance and stars do a clink.
Twinkling lights that join the trance,
Inviting us to join this dance.

In this grand cosmic ball, no strife,
Just joyful rhythms of celestial life.
Time winks at us, oh what a chance,
To join in this hilarious dance!

The Sky's Hidden Narratives

When clouds play chess in the evening air,
The moon pulls pranks, like it doesn't care.
Stars giggle softly at secrets they share,
While comets race by in a flashy flair.

A squirrel named Larry steals the scene,
Wearing a hat that looks quite obscene.
He claims he can count every star on his screen,
But forgets the joke in his own routine.

The planets all dance, but they're out of sync,
Saying, "Join us, Larry! Come have a drink!"
While meteors chat and witty stars wink,
Who knew the cosmos could have such a kink?

So next time you stare at the winking night,
Remember there's laughter beyond your sight.
The universe dreams, but it's light and bright,
With a sprinkle of fun, just to make it right.

Nightfall's Quiet Vigil

A raccoon in shades keeps watch from a tree,
Pondering tea with the owl, full of glee.
Bats don capes, ready for their spree,
While shadows whisper what could never be.

Mice in tuxedos host a grand ball,
Dancing on rooftops, they're having a ball.
The wind plays tunes, a sweet siren call,
And stars clap their hands, having fun with it all.

The moon pulls a prank with a glowing face,
Says, "Every night's just a silly kind of race!"
While fireflies blink in a flickering chase,
Night's laughter echoes through time and space.

So join the revelry, let yourself sway,
Find joy in the odd, in the night's ballet.
When dusk settles down in its whimsical way,
The world holds its breath for the jokes at play.

Passage Through Time and Light

At dawn's early light, the sun yawns aloud,
Sipping on coffee amidst a warm cloud.
Time tricks the clocks, it's feeling quite proud,
While shadows play tag in a dreamy shroud.

A turtle in glasses takes notes for a show,
As lightning bugs zoom past him in a row.
"Why walk when you can glide, don't you know?"
He chuckles and turns, eyes sparkling aglow.

While days slip away on a rollercoaster,
Fish give you tips on becoming a toaster.
The universe giggles, a playful roaster,
Painting nonsense with a star as a poster.

So let's share a laugh while the sun slips away,
With time on our hands, we've more games to play.
In the dance of the cosmos, we find our own way,
And cherish the moments that brighten our day.

A Lullaby of Distant Galaxies

In cradles of stardust, small dreams take flight,
   Whispering secrets till the morning light.
   Nebulas giggle, spinning tales of delight,
     While planets recite an offbeat recite.

   Jellyfish glance at their solar ballet,
Laughing at comets who've lost their own way.
'Hey buddy, get real, don't you mean to play?'
 The stars snicker softly—who needs to obey?

  Time travels sideways in glittering threads,
   Dreaming of astronauts wearing their beds.
While meteors toast with their scrambled eggs,
    Galaxies giggle, tying knotty dreads.

   So let the night hum its nutty refrain,
As laughter cascades like a sweet summer rain.
 In cosmic embrace, we all share the strange,
Where joy's woven tight and nothing's mundane.

www.ingramcontent.com/pod-product-compliance
Lightning Source LLC
Chambersburg PA
CBHW070323120526
44590CB00017B/2791